HORSEPOWER

DRIFT CARS

by Sarah L. Schuette

Reading Consultant:
Barbara J. Fox
Reading Specialist
North Carolina State University

Content Consultant:
Michael Collins
Head of Media Relations, U.S. Drift
Glen Allen, Virginia

Mankato, Minnesota

Blazers is published by Capstone Press,
151 Good Counsel Drive, P.O. Box 669, Mankato, Minnesota 56002.
www.capstonepress.com

Printed in the United States of America

Library of Congress Cataloging-in-Publication Data
Schuette, Sarah L., 1976–
Drift cars / by Sarah L. Schuette.
p. cm.—(Blazers. Horsepower)
Summary: "Describes drift cars, their main features, and how they are raced"—Provided by publisher.
Includes bibliographical references and index.
ISBN-13: 978-1-4296-0826-8 (hardcover)
ISBN-10: 1-4296-0826-9 (hardcover)
1. Automobiles, Racing—Juvenile literature. 2. Drifting (Motorsport)—Juvenile literature. I. Title. II. Series.
TL236.S358 2008
796.7—dc22 2007005405

Editorial Credits
Christopher L. Harbo, editor; Jason Knudson, set designer; Patrick D. Dentinger, book designer; Jo Miller, photo researcher

Photo Credits
Corbis/Ted Soqui, 24–25
Shutterstock/Frederick Nacino, 21; Michael Stokes, 10–11, 14–15, 18–19, 28–29
U.S. Drift/Michael Collins, Brian Eggert & James Dickinson, cover, 4–5, 6–7, 8–9, 12, 13, 14, 16–17, 20, 22–23, 26–27

1 2 3 4 5 6 12 11 10 09 08 07

Table of Contents

DRIFTING

A drift car driver stomps on the gas pedal around the first curve. He cranks the steering wheel and the car drifts sideways.

Motorsports
5
HANKOOK
N.A.S.A.
PRO-RACING
MOTUL
www.jeimportperformance.com

The crowd cheers and screams for more. The driver hits the gas. The car's tires create a huge cloud of smoke. The car slides through another turn.

BLAZER FACT

Drift drivers earn points for staying close to a racing line marked on the course and for creating lots of smoke.

Smoke trails from the car as the practice heat ends. The judges review their notes. The driver with the best drifting style moves on to the final heat.

BLAZER FACT

Drift cars can be two-door coupes or four-door sedans.

DRIVING A DRIFT CAR

Driving a drift car is all about controlling the car. Drivers know how much speed to use and when to brake.

Licencing
Event
D1 NATIONAL CHAMPIONSHIP
GREAT BRITAIN
Licencing
Event
www.v-opt.co.jp
DRIFTWORKS
DRIFTWORKS

Drift cars have highly tuned engines that get very hot. Cooling systems help control the engine temperature during competitions.

BLAZER FACT

Drift car drivers need the right amount of speed around turns. Too much speed causes loss of control and crashes.

Drivers sit in the cockpit. Small steering wheels make it easier for drivers to turn quickly. Drivers pull emergency brakes to lock their tires and drift through turns.

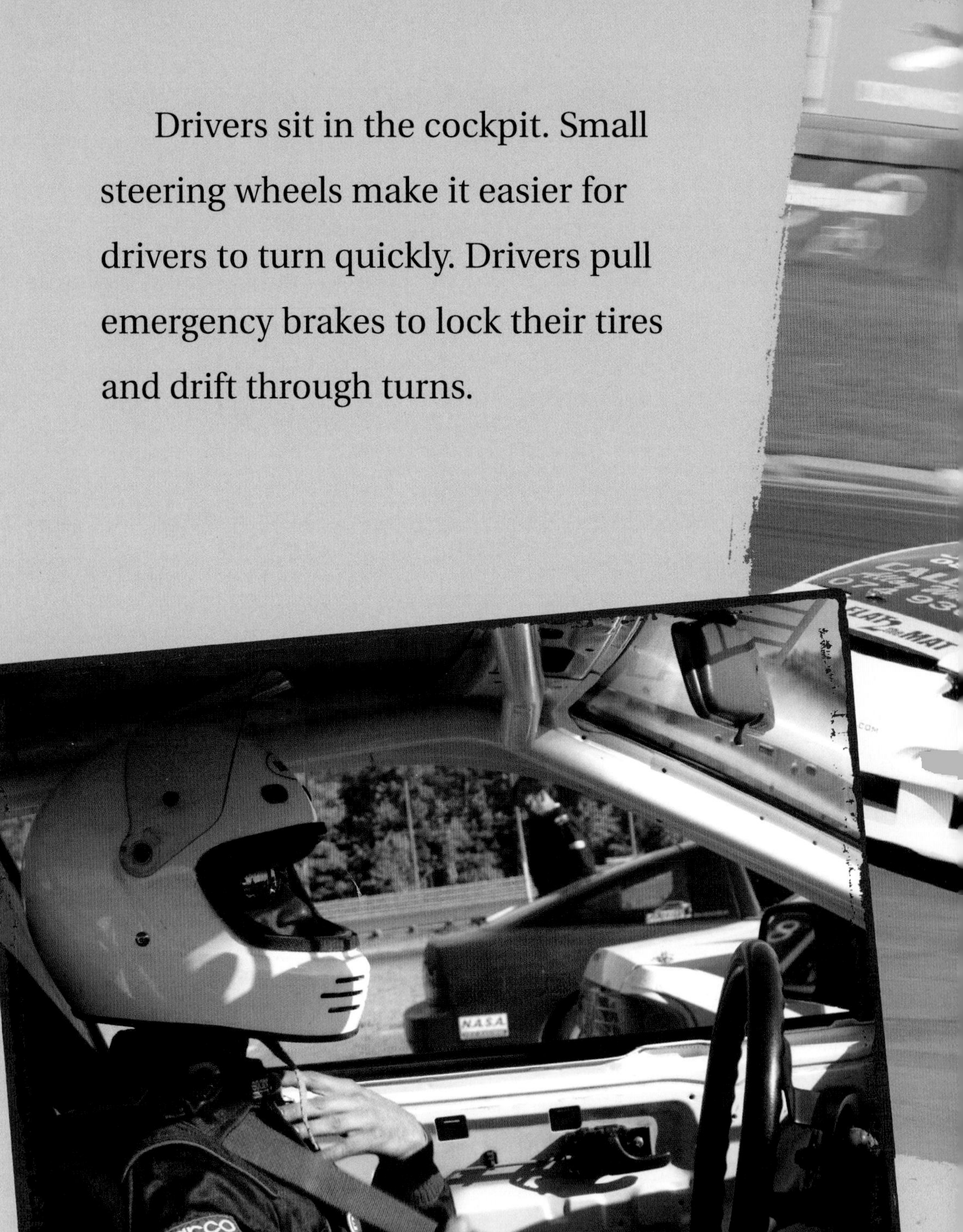

KUMHO
Licencing Event
Ian Coyne
TEIN
BRIDGESTONE
Street Devils.ie
AUTO ZONE
PRODRIFT
GReddy
APEXi
TOYO
HKS
CUSCO

DESIGN AND SAFETY

Drift cars are small and lightweight. They have roll cages for safety. Roll cages are metal frames that protect drivers during crashes.

Roll cage

Drift car tires are over-inflated to reduce traction on the road. Drifting wears tires out quickly. One day of drifting can shred a whole set of tires.

BLAZER FACT

Some drift cars have tires that give off colored smoke when they spin.

The heat drift cars produce can start fires. Drivers wear fireproof suits. Every car has a fire extinguishing system.

BLAZER FACT

Most other race cars have their doors welded shut. Drift car doors open and close so drivers can easily escape a fire.

Drift Car Parts

Rearview mirror

Over-inflated tire

Cockpit
U.S.DRIFT
Roll cage
MA-MOTORSPORTS.COM
Smoking rear tire

A GROWING SPORT

The sport of drifting began in Japan. Drivers practiced on curvy mountain roads. Today, drivers compete on tracks in front of large crowds.

58
A D M
CONCEPT
Ti2000
AUTOBACS
D1 GRAND PRIX SERIES
CUSCO
POTENZA
OGURA CLUTCH
GOODYEAR
FALKEN
DIREZZA
TOYO TIRES
EXMAGIC
i-SHOCK
RS★R
SPORT-SERVICE
ADVAN

U.S.DRIFT
Hankook
MOTUL
MOTUL

Movies, Internet sites, and video games about drifting have made the sport popular worldwide. Drift fans look forward to lots of smoke and expert drifting for years to come.

DRIFTING THROUGH THE TURN!

Licencing
Event
developments
KERR'S TYRES.com
TOYO
YOKOHAMA
HKS
GK
SHAYMAC
PAINTS
www.sidewaysbuff.com

GLOSSARY

cockpit (KOK-pit)—the area in a drift car where the driver sits

cooling system (KOOL-ing SISS-tuhm)—a series of hoses and passages that move water through the engine to keep it cool

drift (DRIFT)—a controlled power slide that happens around a curve

racing line (RAYSS-ing LINE)—the path on the course that a drift driver should follow; drivers receive points for staying close to this line.

roll cage (ROHL KAYJ)—a structure of strong metal tubing in a drift car that surrounds and protects the driver

traction (TRAK-shuhn)—the grip of a car's tires on the ground

weld (WELD)—to join two pieces of metal together by heating them until they melt

READ MORE

Graham, Ian. *The Search for the Ultimate Race Car.* Science Quest. Milwaukee: Gareth Stevens, 2005.

Levy, Janey. *Racing Through History: Stock Cars Then to Now.* Stock Car Racing. New York: Children's Press, 2007.

Morton, Paul. *How to Drift: The Art of Oversteer.* S-A Design Series. North Branch, Minn.: CarTech, 2006.

INTERNET SITES

FactHound offers a safe, fun way to find Internet sites related to this book. All of the sites on FactHound have been researched by our staff.

Here's how:

1. Visit *www.facthound.com*
2. Choose your grade level.
3. Type in this special code **1429608269** for age-appropriate sites. You may also browse by clicking on letters, or by clicking on pictures and words.
4. Click on the **Fetch It** button.

www.FactHound.com®

FactHound will fetch the best sites for you!

INDEX